Abiding Chemistry

Abiding Chemistry

Susan Castillo Street

Aldrich Press

ISBN -13:978-0692415436

Kelsay Books
Aldrich Press
www.kelsaybooks.com

To Jonathan Edmund Street

1943-2012

Acknowledgements

I am grateful to the following publications, in which some of the poems in this collection were first published: *The Missing Slate* ("Question"), *Literature Today* ("Flower Gardens"), "Sailing to the Indies" (*Clear Poetry*), "Nightmare" (*Nutshells and Nuggets*), and "Trees" (*Snakeskin*),"Abiding Chemistry" (*Glasgow Herald*) "*Moments*", "*Tsunami*" and "*Blood Tears*" (*Messages in a Bottle.)*

I would like to express my gratitude to the following: Sally Evans, editor of *Poetry Scotland;* Jo Bell, who created and nurtured the extraordinary poetry group that is 52, and to Norman Hadley; my fellow members of 52 for their intelligent and generous feedback; to the London Conduit Street poets; and to my family on both sides of the Atlantic.

Contents

Abiding Chemistry

Learned scientists have said
energy tends to disperse.

Cigarettes furl into ash.
Strong metals rust. Bombs are transmuted
into rubble. Planes explode
in fireballs. Glowing white bones
leach slowly into dust.

This world endures, though it is poised
in fragile balance, in this elemental dance.

But on a brighter note, they add,
kinetic bonding tends to hold
our molecules together,
keeps us from shimmering
out toward loss.

Perhaps love is its other name,
this abiding chemistry
that binds the fragments close.

Saudade

It's a grey cat winding round our legs, purring purring.
We don't know whether it is rather sweet,
this creature, something to caress, or if it's something
that will trip us, cause us pain and make us curse.

Sometimes it's a feather boa, scratchy,
draped around our neck. There is a glamour
in the way it swirls and flutters in the wind
but we can't wait to cast it off.

It's dark blue, this longing.
Sometimes it pops up as the wail of a trombone,
jazz riff, or aria. It can appear as spirals of fragrance
wafting us away us to other faces, places.

Queen

When I was a little girl
my mother's closet was
a cave of wonders.

In it dresses swirl,
smell of Chanel, caress my face.
One is white lace. Another, midnight satin shimmers,
pools smooth and slick.

On the floor, her shoes point out in spokes
of symmetry, go clock-clock
when I stagger down the hall.

My favourite thing's a hat
made of brown loops with golden spangles
brittle vivacious crown.

Grandmother's House

The house was once a hotel.
My grandfather had it moved on rollers,
timber galleon sailing across the Louisiana prairie
to the place where it now rests.

The air is hot wet silk.
Wisteria wraps its scent
around the columns of the porch.

Flooded rice fields stretch on either side
reflecting sky until it's hard to know
what's sky and what is earth.

When I want to know which way is South
I go there in my mind.

Calcasieu

I remember river summers.
My friends and I, young savages
whooping war, swing out on vines
over coiled brown river water
splash yelling into clouds of rainbow light.

People have been known to drown
in these dark waters when they flail
against the roiling hissing current.
But Louisiana children know the score.

       To keep afloat you just lie back into the river,
       rest into those rippling arms
       ride her currents in white laughter,
       know she bears you where she will.

Flower Gardens

My grandmother's fingers are long.
Her skin, translucent paper.
She teaches me to quilt
and tells me stories.

We piece together hexagons.
Some are slippery yellow satin, worn, I'll bet
by Aunt Marie. A vamp, it's said.
Grandfather's starchy linen jacket
glows snowdrop white in others.
He gave me peppermints.
Tired lilac pansies from Aunt Lola line the edge.
She smelled of lavender, was always ill.
To link them all, paths circle, soft green grass.
The pattern, Flower Garden.

Her hands are lined in silver.

Cookies

Grandmother's kitchen. Linoleum with marble swirls,
floury countertops. She smells of talc and roses.
She cracks eggs into a brown bowl,
butter, sugar, strong Louisiana coffee,
black sugar cane syrup, ginger. Her fingers gnarl swirls in dough,
mould men and women, wheels and hearts. I lick the spoon,
 My tongue bursts in Louisiana sweetness.
Dark spicy smells float into the dusk.

Ginger Holocaust

The legs are the first to go.
I savour amputation.
bite off one foot, then another.

Decapitation comes next. I look the ginger people
in the eye, gnaw a head,
roll a skull on avid tongue.

I save the torso for last:
nip out the hearts
with sharp white teeth.

Ruthie

In our family, we were all
so well behaved. Very ladylike.
We never shouted. Heavens no.
That would be so common.

When cousin Ruthie got pregnant Out of Wedlock,
no one shouted. When my aunts forced her
to give the baby up,(what would people say)
no one raised their voices.

Ruthie bought an old .45
said a soft-voiced thank you sir
to the man who sold it.
So well behaved. Very ladylike.

She went home, sat on her bed,
held the gun, tunneled it with her tongue
Her brains spiraled out in watermelon fragments

At her funeral, no one shouted.
Heavens no. That would be so common.
No one raised their voices.

Them Bones

Don't mess with Southern ghosts.
They sink into black Delta earth.
You cast a clod or two
Just when you hear a satisfying
hollow thunk, it turns out that
the rope gravediggers use
south of the Mason-Dixon line
is springy bungee cord.
up the shadows burst once more
in showers of dark soil.

Arms linked, this Southern chorus line
clatters, silly skellies in a tinkly
xylophone routine:
  how I love you how I love you
  grinning grinning

just when you think that really,
bless their hearts, they're kind of sweet
not too bad to have around, they fold you close
in blue ragtime embrace
rip out your heart
with rotting teeth.

Cord

You lie on my chest
covered in blood and shit,
cord linking us still pulsing hard.

You let out an angry yell,
look up at me, at the blurred figures
that surround us.

In thready whisper, I promise that
I'll always guard you from the dark
because we're linked by sinew, heart to heart.

Condor

Early morning, Colca Canyon. Blue translucent air
shot through with shadow veins.
The valley yawns below,
violet smear of haze.

Buses arrive, disgorge their hordes. Tourists yawn,
shift backpacks, murmur. Then somebody cries, 'There's one!'
We squint, and then the condor rises into view.
He spirals skyward toward the sun. Cameras click.

For one brief moment
far from our jagged world
we stand transfixed, redeemed
by visions of strong gilded wings.

Question

Soft. summer night. In the garden,
my daughter lies back in my arms.
We look up at the stars.

I think of my own mother
folded tight into
her warm dark bed
of Mississippi Delta clay. I wonder where
and why she's gone.

I point up at the sky.
"The Big Dipper" I tell my child.
"A question mark," she says

Daphne's Song

Silly old sod, Apollo,
even though he is a god.
He thinks he can catch me,
cleave me, make me cry out,
spin me skyward in his arms.

But I flee, laughing
see the rough gray scales of bark
that corrugate my limbs. My arms
branch, spiraling toward the sun.
My hair flickers, silver leaves
that shimmer in the wind.

He should know better
than to try to make a myth
of me.

The Walled Garden

You and I will never have
our own walled garden
made of compost and weedkiller
borders and trowels.

Though we did build our own
within four walls
filled with flaming rootless flowers.

still I know
it will outlast
mere stone and earth and air.

Easter Sunday 2003

My garden on Skye. Around me,
meadow, sea and endless light.
It is Easter Sunday.

Here, worlds away from war,
 the fields unfurl
and lambs are daubs of dazzling white.

I think of what we've made of Him,
the Man from Galilee. Black clotted locks
of hair, the sundered hands and feet,
the darkness of grave doctrines.

The image of a child's truncated limbs
flashes like flame
before my eyes.

I conjure up the other Christ
the dancer at the wedding feast,
the alchemist of wine, the healer of
the broken ones, the Lamb of Light
dream of an end

to crucifixions.

Moments

22/11/63
Louisiana afternoon,
high school history class
The football coach comes to the door:
"President Kennedy has been shot in Dallas."
Some of us weep. Others grin and shrug.

04/04/68
Nightfall, small Spanish town.
Televisions flicker, blare:
El reverendo King asesinado en Memphis.
I wonder what has happened to my country.
The screen shifts to flamenco thunder.

25/04/74
Early morning, Portuguese village.
I go into the greengrocers'.
A fat lady dressed in black bursts in:
"There's a Revolution down in Lisbon!"
I buy lettuce, spuds, sweet apples.

31/08/97
Early morning, Scotland.
In the corner shop, tabloids shriek
DIANA KILLED IN PARIS CRASH.
I think, perhaps she will find peace, poor girl
brace myself for avalanche.

11/09/01
Evening, Greek café. I sit and watch
planes crashing into towers
people fleeing in clouds of dust

a man yelling, "Holy shit!"
Again and again and again.
Nothing will ever be the same,

They say that at the moment an atomic bomb explodes
outlines shimmer, colours radiate out
shadows of what was imprinted on the walls
time slows, stops, crystallized
in all its fractures.

Dreich

It's like living in a dishwasher.
Walking in to work, leaning forward, hunched,
I curse. Black horizontal rain swirls around.
Cars splash rainbows, dapple macs.

I remember sunny climes,
think of worn-out chat-up lines.
ask myself: "What's a nice girl like me
doing in a place like this?"

Nightmare

I dream I'm in an airport
running for a plane. Last and final call
for Flight 15. When I reach the gate,
heart drumming in my ears,
the flight has closed.

Heart drumming in my ears
I reach the Gate for Flight 15,
Last and final call. The flight has closed.
I dream I'm in an airport,
running for a plane.

Sailing to the Indies

I hear the sailors mutter.
"This Genovese has led us
to the edge in his mad quest
for gold and souls."

The sea stretches before us,
bolt of blue silk draped
over flat tabletop. In their minds
they look at the horizon, see us sail up to the rim.

go careening down the currents
spiraling into dark space
where monsters lurk and lie in wait for those
who question.

What do these fools know with their false certainties.
The land that lies before us, just beyond Earth's curve,
with endless golden towers and Christ-seeking native souls

is the Indies.

Trees

When I was five, there were
magnolias, branches clotted
with white bursting stars.
Climbing to the top, I float
upon a sea of cloying scent
in Louisiana firefly dusk.

When I was thirty, there were
scrub pines in Portugal, leaning hard
into the cold winds from the sea.
Sitting on the sand, I smell the salt
and dream of solid roots.

Now around me there are
English hornbeams, twisting wild
in winds that barrel off the Channel.
They laugh and sway,
and mock my thoughts of permanence.
They know we aren't here
to stay.

The Alchemy of Stones

January day in Kent. We walk amid graves
that have been here for a thousand years.
It's said that Becket preached here underneath
an ancient yew. Today its branches trace black patterns
against pewter sky. Clots of blackbirds clatter in the cold.

Not easy for somebody from the brave New World
to get her head around the permanence
of English stones. I dream that roots sprout from
my soles, twist deep into the soil,
gnarl tight around bleached bones
shoot tendrils into cavities
where eyes once glittered bright.

I'm warmed by paradox:
   to feel such rootedness and weight
   here in this place where alchemy
   transforms our transitory flesh
   into gray clouds and space and light.

Unexpected Gold

The air of this French town is full of ghosts:
painters, pirates, soldiers, pilgrims
searching for lost souls. Bells peal,
gulls whirl in spirals overhead.

In crowded bistros, avid diners raise their glasses
of rough red. In the harbour, sails are furled tight.
Defiant bristling masts raise fists against the cold,
fend off approaching dark. But still

we walk there hand in hand
beneath the cliffs. Then suddenly late sun breaks through
gray winter dusk and bathes our heads
in waves of unexpected gold.

Tsunami

On the beach, we spread out towels
apply suncream. Around us,
children dig holes, build sandcastles.

Smug, we think of all we've left back home:
Mortgages, the bin collection,
papers full of dismal news.

The sea spreads out like glass,
draws back. On the horizon,
something shifts, begins to rise,
blots out the sun.

Sorry

Sorry I could not save you
though god knows I tried.
I stood guard beside your bed
chatted up nurses
looked surgeons in the eye,
demanded answers.

I sang Cole Porter songs
into your ear. When you didn't wake
I tried the Stones, to no avail.
I told you stories, spoke of family,
invoked saints and angels,
yelled at bureaucrats.

You slept on in beauty
even when I kissed your lips.

I'm sorry all this was in vain.
I'm sorry that I failed
to ward off the dark rider
when the pale horse came near.
I'm sorry that you're gone
while I'm still here.

.

Reflection

You said once as we listened
to the pure young silver voices
of the King's College Choir at Christmas,
you wished you could believe. I saw the yearning.

But I believed in Santa Claus till I was nearly ten.
Now, aging crystal-clanking hippy,
I too yearn for meaning
beyond random loss and chance.

I held you in my arms when you were dying.
Just before the spark went out, I saw
reflected in your eyes, a glimpse of wonder.
and surprise.

Blood Tears

In a gilded church in Italy
There's a statue of Our Lady
her heart transfixed by seven swords.
Local lore maintains

that on a certain day each year,
her tears flow in crimson streams.

Rationalists mock. "As if!"
What do they know.

I have it on the Very Best Authority
that on occasion,
tears ripped from the heart
spurt arterial scarlet, viscous,
leaving acid trails
of blood.

If

If I decided that is was time to move on
nobody loves an Eeyore
particularly in weeping boring widow form
all that black and sorrow

If I were to decide that
a Gentleman Caller would be quite nice
because one does get lonely,
What would be the point?

because there is no one on earth
with whom my imperfections fit
so perfectly as mine did with yours.

Daffodils

It was a cold dark winter
but I planted daffodils on your grave
when sleet was falling.

Now every year in March
there is an explosion
of warm breathing gold.

Bedmates

You always used to steal the duvet.
One day, when we lie together
deep in Sussex soil, you'll be up
to your old tricks.

>Your loam will sprawl over my limbs
>Your roots will weave, tickle my ribs.
>I'll grumble, say turn over for god's sake

But this I know:
Our bones will lie warm together.
>when we're wrapped in that dark quilt.

Wake

The memories are paler now.
It feels as though I'm on a ship,
waving to you on the dock

as you grow smaller, fading
into sea haze
and the wake widens.

Conjuring

To Isabella

You look up at the stars. Black velvet night,
deep in the Sussex Weald. You hold my hand and count
One two free four

If I could buy you the moon
with a gold doubloon
shower you with diamond lights
and garland you with galaxies
shining bright as your brown eyes

I would.

About the Author

Susan Castillo Street is a Louisiana expatriate and academic who lives in the Sussex countryside. She is Harriet Beecher Stowe Professor Emeritus, King's College, University of London, and has published a book of poems titled *The Candlewoman's Trade* (Diehard Press, 2003). Her poems have appeared in *Clear Poetry, The Missing Slate, The Stare's Nest, Nutshells and Nuggets, I Am Not a Silent Poet, Snakeskin, Literature Today,* and *York Mix*, she is also a member of two poetry groups: The Conduit Street Poets (London) and 52.

Printed in Great Britain
by Amazon.co.uk, Ltd.,
Marston Gate.